Let's Barbecue!

From the Reynolds Wrap Kitchens

Favorite Recipes
Subscription Office
5615 W. Cermak Road
Cicero, IL 60650

Favorite Recipes Magazine is published 12 times a year by
Publications International, Ltd., 3841 West Oakton Street,
Skokie, IL 60076

Friends,

The Reynolds Wrap Kitchens are happy to introduce *Let's Barbecue!* — the condensed version of our earlier cookbook, published in 1982, entitled *Barbecue!* We have taken the most popular grilling techniques from *Barbecue!* and packed them into this new version, which is a perfect size for carrying to the grill.

Whether you are looking for a new marinade for meats, a new way to grill fish or just want a no-mess method for grilling ribs, you'll find the instructions in *Let's Barbecue!*

For easy clean-up and even heat distribution, we recommend that you line your charcoal grill with Heavy Duty Reynolds Wrap® aluminum foil before you begin. First lay a sheet of foil long enough to cover the grill from side to side, then criss-cross with another sheet of aluminum foil. Fold over edge of grill and crimp. Cut out openings to conform with grill vents.

The Reynolds Wrap Kitchens have spent hundreds of hours testing and developing these techniques and barbecuing methods. We hope that *Let's Barbecue!* will add hundreds of hours of enjoyment to your barbecue grilling experiences.

Happy grilling,

Carol D. Owen

Carol D. Owen
Director, Consumer Services

Contents

Barbecue Basics

Begin with the basics and barbecuing is easy. Once you know the simple rules of cooking out-of-doors, you're ready for anything over the coals.

Basics start with choosing the right type of equipment for the foods you plan to grill. Today there are at least five basic types of grills, each with a wide variety of special features and options that increase the grill's versatility. Select the type that fits your lifestyle best. Learn to use all of the features on your grill like air vents, adjustable grids and fire pans, and covers to increase your grilling finesse.

Besides the grill, there are accessories and utensils designed to handle even the most delicate foods and make outdoor cooking a cinch. Start with tongs, fork and spatula, then work your way up to the more unusual racks and baskets. Always keep a box of Heavy Duty Reynolds Wrap® aluminum foil and a supply of aluminum foilware for convenient wrapping and disposable containers.

No matter what you plan to cook or what type of grill you own, one of the most important basics is knowing how to build and light the fire. Once you have an evenly burning bed of coals, charcoal cooking the complete meal is simple. Remember to wait for coals that are ashy grey by day or glowing red by night before cooking, then begin your favorite foods by using the proper techniques.

4

Glossary of Terms

Ash Catcher: A pan used to catch ashes from grill. May be inside or outside grill base.

Cover: Found on square cookers and kettles. Helps retain heat inside grill, control flare-ups.

Direct Cooking: Method of grilling foods directly over coals. Heat may be high, medium or low. Best for quick-cooking foods like burgers, chops, steaks, page 16.

Drip Pan: A pan used to catch juices and prevent flare-ups. It can be a foil pan or molded from a sheet of Heavy Duty Reynolds Wrap.

Grid: Stainless steel rack over coals that holds food that is to be cooked.

Hood: Wind screen commonly found on braziers. Meant for protecting fire and food from wind. Some have notches for rotisserie.

Hood can be made from Heavy Duty Reynolds Wrap, page 15.

Ember Cooking: Method of cooking vegetables directly in glowing coals, page 24.

Fire Pan: Holds the coals. Usually a separate container under grid, but in basic grills like hibachis and braziers, the grill itself can be the fire pan.

Indirect Cooking: Method of grilling by arranging coals around or to one side of drip pan. Drip pan is placed directly under food, page 16.

Spit or Rotisserie: Accessory for rotating food over fire. Can be battery or electrically powered.

Vents: Holes in top of hood and bottom of grill with stainless steel or aluminum covers for regulating air flow and temperature of coals.

The Covered Cooker

Round, square or rectangular, the covered cooker is wonderfully versatile. Without the cover, it does everything a brazier does. With the cover, it will roast, steam, smoke and cook whole meals. The cover reduces turning, watching, fussing and flare-ups. It retains heat, so you can use the cooker in any kind of weather.

Look for an adjustable fire pan or grid and vented cover for heat control. The wooden handles make lifting the cover easier and safer.

Three Ways to Use Your Covered Cooker

1. Uncovered. Remove cover and your kettle cooker or square-covered cooker will double as a brazier for searing and quick-cooking.

2. Covered. Add cover to slow-cook larger cuts and whole meals. Adjust heat by raising or lowering fire pan or grid, or opening or closing vents.

3. Rotisserie. Adjust lid to half open for square cookers with rotisserie. Cover can be completely closed also, but be sure vents are open.

The Open Brazier

Any uncovered grill falls into this category. The larger hooded brazier pictured above is one of several open braziers. Some braziers boast half-hoods, covers, and electric or battery-operated rotisseries.

Small tabletop hibachis can also be considered open braziers. When feeding a large crowd, an extra brazier is handy. The heat is regulated by adjusting grid to regulate distance of food from coals. Line the grill with Heavy Duty Reynolds Wrap® for even heat distribution and fast cleanup.

Three Ways to Use Your Brazier

1. Direct Cooking. Line grill with Heavy Duty Reynolds Wrap. Position hot coals directly under food and cook quickly.

2. Rotisserie. Arrange coals around outer edge of fire pan with heavy duty foilware drip pan or foil pan on grid adjusted to lowest position. Remove drip pan when cool.

3. Spit basket. Use flat spit basket to cook smaller foods like salmon steaks, pork steaks, delicate whole fish. Oil rack lightly to prevent sticking.

7

Portable, Tabletop Grills

Many people start barbecuing with a relatively inexpensive portable grill, then progress to a more elaborate one. The simplest grills are small grid-topped models which can be supported on folding or collapsible legs. They're light, easy to clean and store, and come in 12-, 14- and 18-inch sizes.

Great strides have been made in recent years to perfect the portable grill. Choices now run the gamut. Pictured: 1. Tabletop covered kettle, 2. Boat grill, 3. Stand-up hibachi, 4. Fireplace grill, 5. Portable open brazier and 6. Hibachi.

The Gas Grill

The greatest advantage of a gas grill is the convenience. The fire is ready at once, no wait for the "coals" to reach proper cooking temperature. Generally, the initial investment is higher than a charcoal grill. Gas grills now come in smaller portable table-top models as well as larger backyard models.

Lava rock or ceramic briquets are heated by the gas flame, and cook just like charcoal.

9

The Water Smoker

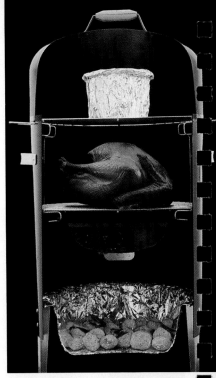

Smoke cooking refers to grilling done in a water smoker-type grill. A water pan placed between food and coals creates a "cloud" around food which permeates meats and vegetables for added smoky flavor. Layering meats and vegetables lets you cook complete meals. Intensify the flavor with a few drops of liquid smoke added to the water pan or sprayed on meat and coals. Since water smoking can take as long as 10 hours, add fresh coals to fire every hour to maintain heat. Remove lid as seldom as possible, each peek adds about 15 minutes to cooking time. Follow manufacturer's directions for cooking times.

Some water smokers have additional stack units to cook several layers of food simultaneously. Gas and electric water smokers are also available.

To ease cleanup, line charcoal pan with Heavy Duty Reynolds Wrap® before lighting the fire.

Add dampened hickory chips to hot coals before cooking food in a water smoker. They add flavor and help create steam that will rise to food. Pour natural liquid hickory smoke into water pan for added flavor.

10

Accessories

The right barbecue accessories are not extras, they're essential. Having the right tool for the right task is safer, as well as more convenient. Barbecue accessories are made from stainless steel wire that is designed to be easy to clean and easy to handle. The right accessories allow you to barbecue food you never expected to cook on the grill. Keep your barbecue accessories in a special place. Hang a utensil rack on your grill so tools are handy.

Utensils should have wooden or thermoplastic handles. Good starter set: two sets of tongs (for coals, food), long-handled fork, spatula, basting brush and utensil holder for hanging.

Hot pads and cooking mitts should be heavy duty and handy. Extra long mitts are ideal for handling hot grills and protecting hands from splatters.

Rotisseries increase versatility of grill. The slow turn is excellent for browning and basting roasts and whole birds.

Charcoal starters are available in electric, liquid and chimney-type. The chimney needs only newspaper. Electric is convenient and fast.

Vinyl covers protect your grill from bad weather. Available in sizes to fit most types of grills. They are an inexpensive way to add years to the life of your grill.

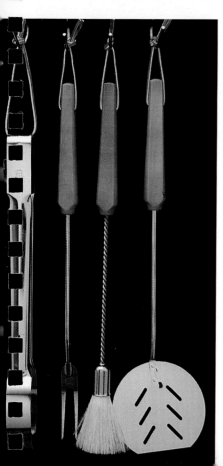

Meat thermometers are available in two styles, quick register and meat probe. They are used to insure rare, medium and well cooked meats on the grill.

Wire accessories add convenience. The Flat Spit Basket, 1, and Tumble Basket, 2, are powered by rotisserie and are ideal for delicate fish. A roast Rack, 3, promotes even cooking, lets you lift out roast easily. Rib Racks, 4, increase cooking area by as much as 50%. Hinged Grill Baskets, 5 and 6, with long handles hold fragile foods securely and make turning easier. Long-handled skewers, 7, are ideal for kabobs.

Disposable aluminum foilware comes in several shapes and sizes. Use it for catching meat juices, cooking cut-up vegetables, warming baked beans and fruit desserts. Ideal for serving directly from the grill.

Baking soda and a water spritzer are ideal for extinguishing flare-ups. Spray water directly at coals or sprinkle baking soda over coals after removing food.

Accessories You Can Make

Reynolds Wrap Hamburger Press. Tear off a sheet of heavy duty aluminum foil 12 inches long. Fold in a series of 1-inch folds to make a 1 × 12-inch strip. Crimp and fold ends together forming a 3-inch ring. Gently pat in ground beef.

Saucepot. Mold three layers of heavy duty aluminum foil around bowl to form desired size. Remove bowl and fold edges down to form tight rim. Use to warm beans, soup, extra sauce. Remove from grill using pot holders in both hands.

Occasionally, even the best-equipped kitchen finds itself without the necessary utensil. That's the time to reach for Heavy Duty Reynolds Wrap.® Not only can aluminum foil be used as a covering or wrap for foods, but since it is so sturdy, it can also be used for making wind screens, hoods, cooking containers and utensils.

Aluminum foil reflects heat, providing an even heat distribution.

Drip Pan or Baking Pan. Tear off 2 sheets of heavy duty aluminum foil. Double fold edges forming 1½- to 2-inch sides. Score and miter corners for strength. Use as drip pan in coals or as baking pan on grid.

How to Make a Foil Hood

Clip off hooks of six or seven coat hangers; straighten. Form a circle using two or more. It should fit just inside the grill.

Loop remaining wire, umbrella fashion, and attach to the circle. Use pliers to twist the ends. Fasten together at top with wire.

Cover wire umbrella frame with Heavy Duty Reynolds Wrap, leaving a small portion loose at top to open and close for temperature control.

How to Make a Foil Wind Shield

Follow directions, left, for making wire umbrella frame. Pull back wire loops on one side of frame to form a half circle. Secure loops in place with wire.

Cover the half frame with Heavy Duty Reynolds Wrap. Place the windguard inside the edge of the grill to block wind and help maintain a steady fire.

Remove aluminum foil when soiled; re-cover frame with clean aluminum foil for reuse.

The Fire

Follow the pyramid method for lighting standard briquets. For instant lighting briquets follow package directions. *An evenly burning bed of coals is the secret to maintaining control over your cookouts.* Many foods require different cooking temperatures, so learn to judge temperature of the coals before you place food on the grill. Always grill in a well ventilated area.

Once the coals have reached the correct cooking temperature, they can be spread for cooking in either the direct or indirect methods. When cooking foods that require longer cooking times, use tongs to add 10 to 12 briquets to edges of burning coals every hour to maintain heat. Different brands of briquets give off varying degrees of heat, so cooking times will always be approximate. Follow techniques on page 18 for controlling the temperature.

How to Arrange a Direct and Indirect Fire

Stack coals in a pyramid to light the fire. Pyramid shape provides enough ventilation for coals to catch. Be sure all coals are touching each other.

Direct cooking. Arrange coals directly under food, extending 1 inch beyond edge of food for direct method.

Indirect cooking. For slow indirect cooking in covered grill, or on rotisserie, place coals to one side of the grill with an aluminum foil drip pan placed under food, pictured above left. For hotter indirect cooking place drip pan in center of coals, pictured above right.

Three Common Types of Starters

Liquid. Sprinkle liquid starter on briquets, allow to soak in for about 45 seconds; light with match. Pre-soaking briquets in a coffee can aids lighting, too.

Wax or jelly. Squeeze over and under briquets. Light briquets before starter evaporates. Shake can before using to loosen wax.

Electric. Nestle into coals. Watch while briquets begin to turn grey. Always remove starter from coals after 8 minutes to avoid burn-outs.

How to Use a Chimney Starter

Place crumpled newspaper in bottom of chimney starter. Leave several newspaper ends sticking out of holes in chimney base. Fill top of chimney with charcoal briquets.

Light newspaper ends with a match. Flames will spread up through chimney to light briquets. Let burn without disturbing for 10 to 15 minutes.

Remove starter when all briquets have begun to turn ashy grey or are glowing by night. Use insulated hot pads when picking up chimney. Spread coals in single layer with tongs.

17

How to Know if Coals are Ready

Ashy grey coals by day mean fire is hot and it's time to begin cooking. For even cooking, never grill while some coals are still black.

Glowing red by night also says it's time to cook. As temperature falls at night, keep coals closer together to maintain heat. Tap ash off as coals burn down to maintain heat.

Thermometer on top of dome lid of smoker grill indicates the internal temperature. Keep an eye on it throughout cooking.

How to Adjust Heat

Control Air Flow. Vent holes in a covered grill control air flow throughout. To raise the temperature, open vents fully. To lower the temperature, close halfway. To snuff out coals, close vents entirely.

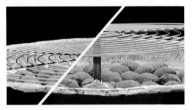

Control Grid Height. Distance of food from coals will affect cooking temperatures. Lower the grid for more intense heat and quick cooking. Raise the grid for longer, slower cooking without charring.

Control Closeness of Coals. In addition to distance, closeness of coals to each other affects temperature. To lower temperature, spread coals further apart. To increase heat, bank closer together and tap ash.

Judge Fire Temperature

Judge temperature by cautiously holding your hand, palm side down, over coals at grid level. Count the seconds that you can hold the position.

Fire Temperature Chart

Seconds Hand Held Over Fire	Fire Temperature is:
5 seconds	Low
4 seconds	Medium
3 seconds	Medium-High
2 seconds	Hot

Temperatures to Begin Cooking

Heat	Temp. of Coals	Grid Height	Foods
Low	Med.-Low	High	**Beef:** Roasts; **Desserts; Seafood:** Clams, Oysters, skewered
Medium	Med.-Low	Medium	**Beef:** Cubes; **Lamb:** Cubes, Leg; **Lobster; Pork:** Chops, Cubes, Roasts; **Poultry:** Pieces, Whole birds; **Pre-Baked Fruit Pies; Sausages:** Bologna, Hot dogs (Franks), Pork links (precooked); **Vegetables**
High	High	Low	**Beef:** Burgers; **Pork:** Ribs; **Toasting:** Rolls

Note: To retain juiciness, thick cuts of meat should be seared on high, then cooked at medium or low heat to finish.

19

Grilling Techniques

Open Brazier Method

This cutaway grill illustrates the simplest method of barbecuing. The open brazier relies on direct heat. It is excellent for foods requiring quick searing like steaks, burgers, chops, hot dogs. Think of it as broiling outdoors. *Wait until coals die down to the ashy grey stage before placing food on grid.*

Since many open braziers come without grids for controlling temperature, learn to use the hand hold test for judging temperature of coals. Smaller braziers like hibachis and picnic grills require fewer coals so don't overload. And in case of fat flare-ups, have a water pistol handy. With open brazier cooking, foods should be no more than 5 inches from the coals.

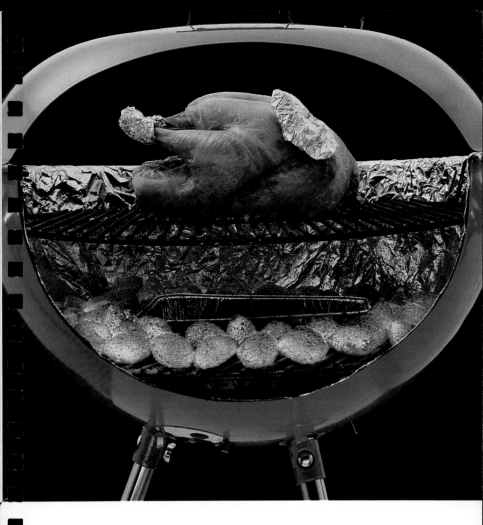

Covered Cooking

This method, also called dry smoking, is similar to roasting in an oven, only with charcoal as the source of heat. Food is cooked by heat reflected from the cover, as well as with heat from the coals. Food is surrounded by a uniform, controlled heat that substantially cuts cooking time and allows meat to maintain its natural juiciness and flavor. The covered cooker is excellent for whole birds, roasts, whole fish and vegetables.

As a technique, covered cooking is one of the most versatile methods. It may be done in a square, rectangular or kettle cooker. The indirect method is often applied to covered cooking. Plan whole meals from main dish to dessert for the covered cooker.

Rotisserie Cooking

Plug-in or battery-powered rotisserie gives old-fashioned done-to-a-turn flavor to meat, fish and poultry. For most even cooking, be sure meat is balanced and secure on spit. Readjust if needed. Surest grip may involve placing prongs at one end at right angles to prongs at other end. Place aluminum foil drip pan to front of grill to catch meat juices. For detailed rotissing instructions on poultry, see page 58; for pork, page 44; for beef, page 37.

Rotisserie Techniques

Spit basket. Use spit basket for slowly cooking delicate fish and vegetables. Lightly oil basket before adding food to avoid sticking. Brush food with butter or margarine for moistness.

Drip pan. Keep fat out of the fire and catch drippings with a drip pan shaped from a double thickness of Heavy Duty Reynolds Wrap,® page 14.

Small birds. Mount two small birds rather than one large bird on spit for easier handling and quicker cooking times. Butt birds together legs to shoulders for compactness and balance.

Foil shielding. Avoid charred wings or legs. Secure them with string before spitting birds. Wrap aluminum foil around wing tips and leg ends to prevent burning.

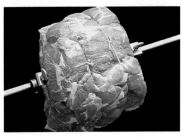

Balancing. Look for evenly shaped cuts of meat to ensure even roasting. See page 58 for balance test.

Basting. Apply marinades and sauces with a long-handled brush. Baste frequently.

23

Ember Cooking

Cooking vegetables directly in the coals gives them a wonderful woodsy flavor.

Always oil skins lightly before cooking. For some thinner-skinned types, Drugstore Wrap in Heavy Duty Reynolds Wrap.® Cooking times vary according to temperature of coals. To reduce charring of vegetable skins, wrap in aluminum foil and cook over low temperature using minimum number of coals to surround vegetables. Prick with fork to test doneness.

Onions. Bury in coals; cook until black and soft to fork pressure, about 1¼ hours. Use tongs to remove onion to cool surface.

Slip off charred skin and discard. Onion inside will be smoky-delicious! Eat while hot.

Potatoes. Rub scrubbed, dry potato skins with oil or margarine. Drugstore Wrap in heavy duty aluminum foil. Cook 45 to 55 minutes until soft when pricked. Turn occasionally.

Squash. Nestle whole butternut or acorn squash in hot coals. Turn occasionally. Roast 45 to 60 minutes. Open, remove seeds; butter. Season with nutmeg, mustard or brown sugar.

Corn. Remove silk; soak corn-in-husks in ice water for 30 minutes. Shake off excess water. Roast corn with or without aluminum foil directly in coals 35 to 45 minutes; turn often.

Wrapping Techniques

Choosing the right fold for foil-barbecuing food calls for common sense. Foods which create a lot of steam or expansion (like popcorn) should have a loose Bundle Wrap. Foods which require frequent turning will fare better in Drugstore Wrap.

How to Bundle Wrap

Center odd shapes and some types of moist food on a square of heavy duty aluminum foil that's roughly three times the size of the food.

Bring four corners up together into a pyramid shape. Fold opening together loosely. Be sure to allow room for heat circulation and expansion.

Seal by folding over ends and pressing to package. Keep upright to avoid leakage. Wrap is especially good for irregular-shaped foods.

How to Drugstore Wrap

Place food in center of oblong piece of heavy duty aluminum foil large enough to allow for folding at top and sides.

Bring two sides together above food; fold down in a series of locked folds, allowing for heat circulation and expansion.

Fold short ends up and over again and crimp close to package to seal. This reduces leakage and cooks food evenly.

Marinades, Sauces & Butters

Enhance foods with marinades, sauces and butters. Marinades stretch budgets by tenderizing and flavoring inexpensive cuts of meat. Marinades work by penetrating meat fibers and should always contain an acid or alcohol base such as vinegar, fruit juice, wine or beer.

Look for flavor balance in a marinade. Marinades can be cooked or uncooked. Cooked marinades should be chilled before adding to meat. Pour in enough marinade to immerse meat halfway, then cover dish.

How to Marinate

Marinate in refrigerator overnight, but no longer than 24 hours. Turn occasionally. Cubed meats should be marinated only 2 to 3 hours. Cover.

Brush both sides of the meat with extra marinade during cooking. Use an aluminum foil saucepot, to keep the marinade warm.

Herb Butter on Barbecued Chicken, page 29

Marinade Chart

Use ½ cup of marinade for each pound of meat.

Type	Combine the following ingredients	Use On
Apple Tarragon 2 cups	1 cup apple cider, ⅓ cup vinegar, ⅓ cup sliced green onions with tops, ¼ cup vegetable oil, 3 tablespoons honey, 2 tablespoons steak sauce, 1½ teaspoons tarragon leaves, 1 teaspoon salt and ¼ teaspoon freshly ground pepper. Bring to a boil, simmer uncovered 20 min. Chill.	Chicken Lamb
Beer 2 cups	1 can (12 oz.) beer, ½ cup vegetable oil, 2 tablespoons cider vinegar, 1 small onion, thinly sliced, 2 cloves garlic, minced, 1 teaspoon salt and ½ teaspoon freshly ground pepper.	Beef
Curry Apple 1 cup	1 cup applesauce, 2 tablespoons lemon juice, 2 teaspoons curry powder, 1 teaspoon salt and ¼ teaspoon pepper.	Lamb
Mint Honey 1 cup	⅔ cup dry white wine, ⅓ cup honey, 1 tablespoon vinegar, 1 clove garlic, minced, 1½ teaspoons chopped fresh mint and 1 teaspoon salt.	Lamb
Onion Soup 1 cup	1 envelope onion soup mix, ½ cup vegetable oil, ¼ cup cider vinegar, 1 teaspoon sugar and 1 teaspoon Worcestershire sauce.	Beef
Pineapple 1½ cups	1 can (6 oz.) or ¾ cup unsweetened pineapple juice, ½ cup dry sherry, 2 tablespoons brown sugar, 1 clove garlic, minced and ½ teaspoon rosemary leaves.	Pork
Teriyaki 1½ cups	½ cup soy sauce, ⅓ cup dry sherry, ⅓ cup firmly packed brown sugar, ¼ cup vinegar, 2 tablespoons vegetable oil, 1 clove garlic, minced and ½ teaspoon ginger.	Beef Chicken Pork Seafood
White Wine 2 cups	¾ cup dry white wine, ¼ cup lemon juice, ¾ teaspoon salt, ½ teaspoon pepper and ½ teaspoon dry mustard.	Fish

27

Sauces

Sauces are used to flavor foods. They are brushed on during cooking, and unlike marinades, have no tenderizing qualities. Sauces come in a range of flavors, from sweet to savory.

Sugar-based glazes and sauces will burn quickly and should be brushed on during the last 15 minutes of grilling. Keep sauces within easy reach of food that you are preparing.

Sauce Chart

Type	Method	Use On
Apple Curry 1⅔ cups	In a saucepan, combine 1 jar (10 oz.) apple jelly, ⅓ cup dry white wine, ¼ cup sliced green onions with tops, 2 tablespoons prepared mustard, ½ teaspoon salt, ½ teaspoon curry powder and ½ teaspoon freshly ground pepper. Heat until jelly has melted, stirring occasionally.	Chicken Lamb
Apricot Ginger 1½ cups	Combine 1 jar (12 oz.) apricot preserves, 3 tablespoons cider vinegar, 2 tablespoons melted butter, ½ teaspoon ground ginger and ½ teaspoon salt.	Chicken Pork
Hot and Spicy 2 cups	In a saucepan, combine 1 can (8 oz.) tomato sauce, ⅓ cup vinegar, ⅓ cup packed brown sugar, 2 tablespoons prepared mustard, ½ cup chopped onion, 1 clove garlic, finely chopped and 1 tablespoon chili powder. Bring to boil; simmer 5 min.	Chicken Hamburger Pork Steak
Cucumber 1¼ cups	Combine ¾ cup peeled, diced cucumber, ¼ cup dairy sour cream, ¼ cup mayonnaise, 1 tablespoon sliced green onion, 1 teaspoon grated lemon peel and ¼ teaspoon dill weed. Cover and refrigerate to blend flavors.	Chicken Fish Pork
Tangy Beer ⅔ cup	Combine ⅓ cup chili sauce, ¼ cup beer, 2 teaspoons prepared horseradish, ½ teaspoon sugar, ½ teaspoon salt, ¼ teaspoon pepper, ½ teaspoon instant minced onion and ¼ teaspoon dry mustard.	Hamburger Steak

Butters

Plan an assortment of butters so guests can choose their own. Serve butter two ways: melted and brushed on hot, or room temperature and spread with knife. Always soften butter to room temperature before adding flavorings or use margarine. Tub-type margarines are ready at once. Add butter to second side of meat during last stages of cooking to prevent burning.

Butter Chart

Type	Method: Combine the following ingredients	Use On
Blue Cheese	¼ cup softened butter, ½ cup crumbled blue cheese, 1 clove garlic, minced, 1 tablespoon sliced green onions.	Hamburgers Steak
Cheese Herb	½ cup softened butter, 3 tablespoons Parmesan cheese, 1 tablespoon finely chopped parsley, ½ teaspoon basil leaves, ¼ teaspoon garlic powder.	Corn Zucchini Vegetables
Cinnamon Sugar	¼ cup softened butter, ¼ cup firmly packed brown sugar, ½ teaspoon cinnamon, ¼ teaspoon nutmeg, ½ teaspoon grated lemon peel, 1 teaspoon lemon juice.	Bread Apple or banana bundles
Garlic	½ cup softened butter, 1 tablespoon finely chopped parsley, 1 teaspoon garlic powder.	Shrimp Sliced bread Steak
Herb	½ cup softened butter, 2 tablespoons sliced green onions, 2 tablespoons chopped parsley, ½ teaspoon tarragon leaves, ¼ teaspoon salt.	Chicken Fish Mushrooms Vegetables
Mustard	½ cup softened butter, ¼ cup Dijon mustard, 1 tablespoon sliced green onions with tops, ¼ teaspoon garlic powder, ¼ teaspoon pepper, dash Worcestershire sauce.	Beef Duck
Parsley Orange	½ cup softened butter, 1 tablespoon grated orange peel, 1 tablespoon orange juice, 1 tablespoon honey, 2 teaspoons chopped parsley.	Chicken Duck Lamb

Beef

Barbecuing beef is one of the best ways to bring out its hearty, rich flavor. Charcoal grilled beef should be crispy on the outside and juicy on the inside. Sear quickly over hot coals to lock in juices. Finish over medium to medium-hot coals.

Barbecuing the Perfect Burger

For regular size burgers, use open brazier; do meat-loaf size "burgers" in a covered cooker.

For juicy burgers, choose higher fat cuts, chuck or sirloin. Round (about 15% fat) is lower-calorie. Try some wonderful combinations: onion, avocado, cheese condiments, soy sauce, horseradish, you name it! To prevent meat from sticking to grid, oil rack lightly.

31

How to Barbecue Burgers

Pack ground beef lightly into aluminum foil press. Overhandling causes tough burgers. See page 13. Make ½-inch (2 oz.) to 1-inch (4 oz.) thick patties.

Rare burgers need 4 minutes of searing on second side over medium coals.

Arrange burgers 4 to 6 inches from hot coals. Spritz flare-ups with water mister.

Medium burgers need 6 more minutes on second side if ½ inch thick, 7 more minutes if 1 inch thick.

Sear ½-inch thick burgers 2 minutes on first side; 1-inch thick burgers 3 minutes. Turn only once and cook until done.

Well done burgers may need 12 more minutes on open brazier after searing. Cut slit in center to judge doneness.

Brush sauce on burger while searing, then again after turning, if desired.

Place buttered buns, cut side down, around edges of grill to toast. Guests can add their own toppings as desired.

Hamburger Variations

Mix With Beef	Stuff Your Burger*	Top With	Bun
Taco sauce	Monterey Jack cheese with jalapeño peppers	Sour cream, avocado slices, cooked bacon	Sesame bun, butter
Chopped onions, salt, pepper	American cheese	Heated, canned chili	Kaiser roll, butter
Salt, pepper	Capers, cooked bacon	Spinach leaves	English muffin
Catsup, mustard, salt, pepper	Sliced kosher pickles	Swiss cheese	Onion bagel, mustard
Worcestershire sauce, salt, pepper	Blue cheese	Chopped tomato, sliced onion, cucumber, leaf lettuce	Kaiser roll, Dijon mustard
Chopped mushrooms, basil leaves	Mozzarella cheese	Pizza sauce, chopped olives	Italian bread, butter

*Note: Stuff by placing ingredients between two ½-inch uncooked patties. Seal edges and grill as directed. Stuffers may be used as toppers if unstuffed hamburgers are preferred.

33

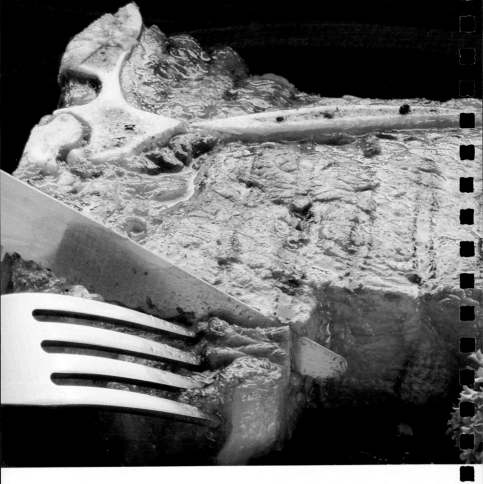

Steak

Who can resist a hot, sizzling barbecued steak! A steak for barbecuing should be at least 1 to 2 inches thick. For a crowd, do one large steak or individual steaks to taste. Try marinating less expensive steaks such as chuck, round and flank for great flavor. For extra special flavor, top a steak with seasoned butters.

How to Barbecue Steaks

Trim excess fat. Slash remaining fat just to (not into) meat. Place on grill about 4 inches from hot coals to sear.

Steak Chart

Cut and Thickness	First Side	Second Side
Club, Rib, Rib-eye, T-bone, Porterhouse, Sirloin 1¼-inch	Sear on high, direct heat. 3 to 5 min.	Medium to low heat.* Rare: 8 min. Medium: 10 min. Well: 12 to 15 min.
Top round, Chuck 1¼-inch	Marinate and/or tenderize. Sear on high, direct heat. 5 to 8 min.	Medium to low heat.* Rare: 7 to 10 min. Medium: 12 min. Well: 15 min.
Flank steak ½-inch	Score both sides; marinate. Sear on high, direct heat. 5 min.	High direct heat. 5 min.
London broil (1st cut top round) 2-inch	Marinate and/or tenderize. Sear on high, direct heat. 8 min.	Medium to low heat.* Rare: 20 min. Medium: 22 min.

*To lower temperature, increase distance from fire and cover grill, if desired.

Turn the steak using long-handled tongs. (Do not use a fork or juices will escape.)

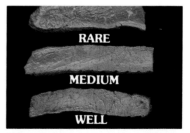

RARE

MEDIUM

WELL

Check doneness by slitting close to bone. Carve thin slanting slices for tenderness.

Beef Roasts

How to Barbecue Roasts

Use indirect method or rotisserie over a constant medium to low heat to barbecue beef roasts. Shield bony tips with aluminum foil to prevent burning. Check doneness with a meat thermometer. For easier carving, remove the roast from the grill and let it rest on a carving board about 15 minutes before slicing.

Choose a well-marbled, evenly contoured roast. Trim so fat is no more than ½ inch thick. Cook either on rotisserie or in covered cooker.

Beef Roast Chart

Use medium to low, indirect heat.

Cut and Weight	Time	Internal Temp.
Beef rib roast 4 to 6 lbs.	Rare: 14 to 16 min./lb. Medium: 16 to 20 min./lb.	140°F. 160°F.
Boneless beef roast: **Round rump, Round tip, Chuck cross-rib pot roast** 4 to 6 lbs.*	Rare: 20 to 22 min./lb. Medium: 23 to 25 min./lb.	140°F. 160°F.
Fresh beef brisket, Flat half, boneless** 4 to 7 lbs.	4½ to 6 hours	140°F.

*Marinate roast 4 hours or overnight in refrigerator.
**Use charcoal water smoker. Follow manufacturer's instructions.

Rotisserie. Tie roast into uniform shape. Push spit lengthwise through meat; fasten with holding forks. Place aluminum foil drip pan in coals beneath and in front of roast.

Covered Cooker. Place roast into rack and place on grid. Use aluminum foil drip pan and grill by the indirect method. Add cover or aluminum foil hood and grill until done.

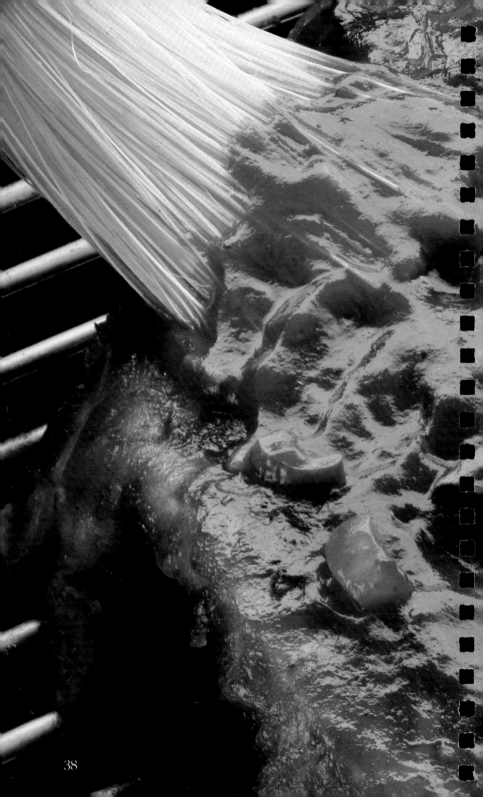

Pork

Teriyaki Marinade on pork chops, page 27

Barbecuing Pork

The slow roast of a covered kettle or water smoker is ideal for barbecuing pork. The best pork is grilled slowly over low to medium coals. Pork is often a more economical choice for feeding crowds, so don't overlook smoky pork chops, whole pork roasts, seasoned pork burgers, racks or rotisserie spits full of ribs when planning an outdoor menu.

How to Prepare Pork Chops

Slash the fat on pork chops just to the meat. This prevents curling. Trim off any excess fat.

40

General Tips on Grilling Pork

Pork manufacturers are processing leaner meat. To insure best results grill slowly 4 to 6 inches from medium to low coals. Cook until juices run clear, and meat is no longer pink.

Pork Chops, Steaks and Burgers Chart

Cut and Size	Time	Method
Ground Pork Burgers ½ inch thick	15 to 20 min.	**For all cuts:** make a bed of medium to low coals.
Pork Kabobs 1¼-inch cubes	15 to 20 min.	(High, searing heat will toughen pork and smoked ham.) Grill first side about
Rib, Loin Chops ¾ to 1 inch thick	20 to 30 min.	half recommended time over direct heat or until browned. Turn and sea-
Shoulder Blade Steaks ¾ to 1 inch thick	25 to 35 min.	son or baste with sauce, if desired. Grill until done,
Smoked Loin Chops 1 inch thick	15 to 20 min.	but still juicy and tender. (Do not overcook or pork will be dry and tough.)
Loin Chops, stuffed	45 min.	For stuffed pork chops use a covered grill.

Stuff a 1½-inch thick pork chop with a savory stuffing. Cut a pocket from rib side to center of chop, cutting parallel to surface.

Marinate pork not so much for tenderness as for deep-down flavor. Brush on marinade during cooking, also.

Pork Burger Chart

Use medium, direct heat.

Type	Season Pork With	Stuff Center With
American	Liquid smoke, chopped onion, salt, pepper	American cheese
Chinese	Chopped fresh parsley, garlic powder, sage, salt, pepper	Sliced water chestnuts
Italian	Parmesan cheese, pepper	Sliced mushrooms
Mexican	Chopped green chilies, salt, pepper	Monterey Jack cheese
Polynesian	Soy sauce, salt, pepper	Pineapple ring, chopped green pepper

Note: Buy lean ground pork or ask your butcher to grind pork from a Boston pork shoulder roast.

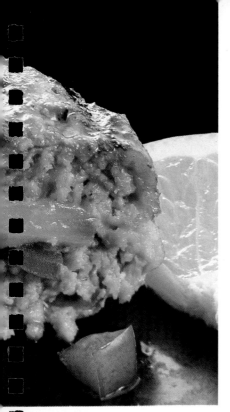

Polynesian-Stuffed Pork Burger; chart below

Baste With
Combined catsup and prepared mustard
Teriyaki sauce
Pizza sauce
Taco sauce
Pineapple juice

How to Prepare Ground Pork for Barbecuing

Combine ¼ pound ground beef to every pound ground pork for juiciest burgers. Pick seasoning from chart below.

Season ground pork with liquid smoke, onion, garlic, sage, pepper, lemon, shredded cheese, mustard or your idea.

Stuff filling between two ½-inch thick uncooked patties. Seal edges and grill as directed on chart, page 41.

43

Pork Roasts

Pork roasts, boneless or bone-in, taste delicious when barbecued. They cook slowly and evenly in covered grills, water smokers, or on rotisseries. For easy carving, buy a boned, rolled loin. Cook all pork roasts over low to medium heat to an internal temperature of 170°F for juicy, tender pork. Let rest for 15 minutes before carving.

Pork Roast Chart

Use medium to low, indirect heat.

Type/Size Roast	Time	Internal Temp.	Method
Bone-in: Pork loin, Pork butt, Pork shoulder 3 to 5 lbs.	15 to 18 min./lb.	170°F	Use rotisserie or cover grill.
Boneless: Pork loin, Pork butt, Pork shoulder 3 to 5 lbs.	22 to 25 min./lb.	170°F	Use rotisserie or cover grill.
Fully Cooked Ham 3 to 5 lbs.	15 to 18 min./lb.	140°F	Cover grill.
Smoked Ham Half Cook-before-eating 5 to 7 lbs.	22 to 25 min./lb.	160°F	Remove rind and score fat diagonally before cooking. Stud with cloves if desired. Cover grill.
Rib Crown Roast unstuffed 7 to 8 lbs.	13 to 16 min./lb.	170°F	Place in baking pan directly on grid. Cover grill. Use direct, medium to low heat.

Two Methods for Grilling Pork Roasts

1. Rotisserie. Buy a roast that's a good size and shape to skewer. Boned roasts work best. Be sure prongs hold roast securely.

2. Roasting. Indirect heat in a covered cooker is another alternative for barbecuing roasts. A light basting is desirable.

Flavor roast by tossing damp hickory chips, garlic cloves or onion skins onto coals. With cover down flavor permeates meat.

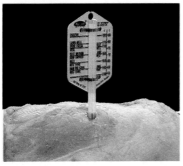

Use a meat thermometer to tell doneness of roasts. Insert thermometer into thickest part of meat not touching bone or fat.

Use a roast rack when barbecuing a roast in a covered grill. It allows for even cooking and simplified lifting.

45

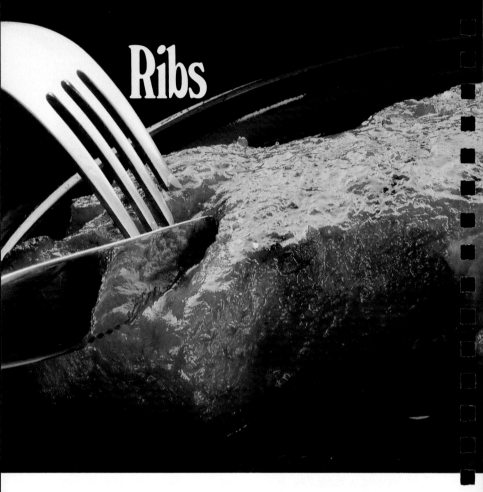

Ribs

The most famous "down home" barbecue recipe is likely to be one for ribs. Succulent and crusty, ribs make finger-lickin' eating. The three main kinds of ribs are spareribs, country-style ribs and back ribs. Spareribs are often a bit more expensive per pound. Fortunately, the same sauces work equally well with all sorts of ribs. Find your favorite — and enjoy!

How to Steam Ribs

Steam ribs before grilling to render out fat. Place ribs in double thickness of Heavy Duty Reynolds Wrap® with 2 tablespoons water. Drugstore Wrap. Seal tightly.

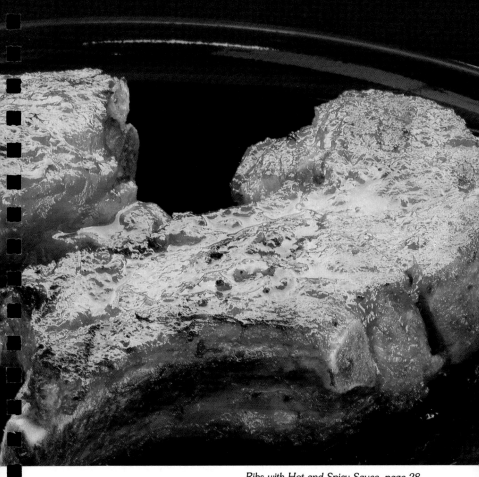

Ribs with Hot and Spicy Sauce, page 28

Place aluminum foil packet with ribs over the hot coals. Grill for ¾ to 1 hour in either a covered cooker or on an open brazier. Do not open the packet during steaming.

Lift packet from grill to table. Drain fat. Remove ribs from aluminum foil packet. Finish either on open brazier or in covered grill.

How to Grill Ribs

Spareribs. Cook a rack of spareribs on the rotisserie by threading it accordion-style on the spit.

Country-Style Ribs. Grill country-style ribs upright in a rib rack. Close grill cover for best results.

Baby Back Ribs. Cut slab into servings of four ribs each. Place in rotisserie basket and let them tumble as they cook.

Open Brazier. Place drained ribs directly on grid. Brush during cooking with sauce or marinade. Apply sweet sauces during last 15 minutes to avoid burning.

Covered Grill. Grill drained ribs either indirectly on grid over drip pan, pictured above left, or place in rib rack, pictured above right. Baste occasionally during cooking with long-handled brush. Cook with cover down.

Rib Chart

Allow 1 to 2 servings per pound of ribs.

Type	Time	Method
Baby Back Ribs (cut in serving-size sections)	Foil Bake: ¾ hr. Grill: ½ to 1 hr.	Foil-bake over high, direct heat. Remove from aluminum foil. Coat well with barbecue sauce. Place in rotisserie basket. Use medium-low, indirect heat. Baste several times with barbecue sauce.
Country-Style Ribs (cut in serving-size sections)	Foil Bake: 1 hr. Grill: ½ to 1 hr.	Foil-bake over high, direct heat. Remove from aluminum foil. Season with salt, pepper, and garlic powder. Place on grid. Cover grill. Use medium-low, indirect heat. Baste with barbecue sauce.
Spareribs	Foil Bake: 1 hr. Grill: ½ to 1 hr.	Foil-bake over high, direct heat. Remove from aluminum foil. Place on grid or in rib rack. Use medium-low, direct heat. Baste with barbecue sauce.
Beef Ribs		Foil-bake over high, direct heat. Remove from aluminum foil. Season with salt, pepper, and garlic powder. Place on grid. Cover grill. Use medium-low, indirect heat. Baste with barbecue sauce.

Sausages

There are as many different types of sausages as there are nationalities. The kind and amount of processing that a sausage receives determines its storage and cooking requirements. Always check the label or with the butcher to see if sausage is cooked or uncooked.

As a rule, fresh sausage requires precooking to remove some of the natural fat. Precooked fresh sausage can then be grilled over a drip pan and medium, indirect heat. Fully cooked sausage may be grilled over medium, direct heat without a drip pan or precooking.

How to Barbecue Sausages

Precook fresh sausages with 1 or 2 tablespoons of water. Drugstore Wrap. Steam over medium coals 10 minutes, pictured above left. Finish cooking over an aluminum foil drip pan to catch drippings and prevent flare-ups, pictured above right. For best results, turn often, until evenly browned on all sides.

Split large fully cooked sausages in half lengthwise, cutting down but not all the way through. Grill over medium, direct heat 10 to 15 minutes, turning frequently.

Grill fully cooked sausages directly over medium coals, turning frequently. Cook until browned and heated through.

Serve a mixed grill for lunch. Precook fresh sausages over fire first; add fully cooked sausages during last 15 minutes. Nice menu additions are hot German potato salad, cooked in aluminum foil on the grill, or chilled, seasoned sauerkraut.

51

Lamb

Barbecued lamb is distinctive when you want an extra special cookout. It has just the right amount of marbling to let grilling proceed smoothly, and the flavor of lamb is enhanced by charcoaling. Lamb can be transformed with seasonings and marinades of various kinds or grilled "as is" with a sprig of fresh mint.

How to Cook Lamb

Chops/Steak. Marinate 4 hours or overnight for extra flavor. Grill chops over medium, direct heat.

Lamb Chart

Cut	Time	Method
Boneless loin, Shoulder roasts 4 to 5 lbs.	Rare (140°F): 20 min./lb. Medium (160°F): 22 min./lb. Well Done (170°F): 25 min./lb.	Grill in covered cooker or rotisserie over medium coals. Place aluminum foil drip pan under meat to catch drippings for gravy. Brush frequently with favorite sauce.
Chops, Steaks ¾ to 1 inch thick	13 to 16 min.	Place on grid. Use medium, direct heat.
Kabobs from leg 1¼-inch cubes	13 to 16 min.	Marinate 4 hours or overnight in refrigerator. Thread cubes on skewers. Place on grid. Use medium, direct heat. Baste with sauce, see page 28.
Leg of lamb, boned, rolled and tied 4 to 5 lbs.	Same times as Shoulder roasts, above.	Marinate lamb. Place on grid. Cover grill. Use medium, indirect heat. Turn and baste occasionally with marinade.

52

Cubes. Marinate lean lamb cubes from the leg or shoulder and skewer with vegetables. Grill over medium, direct heat.

Roasts. Barbecue large cuts like boneless leg, shoulder and loin in covered grill or rotisserie. Use medium, indirect heat; baste often.

Lamb Sauces and Seasonings Chart

Type	Method
Barbecue Sauce	Combine ⅓ cup catsup, ¼ cup chili sauce, 1 tablespoon finely chopped onion, 1 tablespoon finely chopped green pepper, 1 tablespoon brown sugar, and 1 tablespoon soy sauce. Spread on lamb during last 10 to 15 minutes of cooking.
Italian Baste	Baste meat with dry white wine while grilling. Combine ¼ cup dry bread crumbs, 2 tablespoons Parmesan cheese, 1 clove garlic, finely chopped, ½ teaspoon basil leaves, ½ teaspoon salt and dash pepper. Pat on meat halfway through cooking time. Continue basting with wine and pat on more crumb mixture, if needed.
Mustard Dill Sauce	Combine ½ cup mayonnaise, ½ cup dairy sour cream, 2 tablespoons sliced green onion, 2 teaspoons Dijon mustard, 1 teaspoon Worcestershire sauce, 1 teaspoon dill weed, and ½ teaspoon salt. Cover; refrigerate several hours. To serve, spoon over grilled lamb.
Pineapple Chutney Sauce	In a saucepan, combine 1 can (15¼ oz.) crushed pineapple, ½ cup chutney, ¼ cup firmly packed brown sugar, ¼ cup butter, 1 teaspoon ground ginger and ½ teaspoon salt. Bring mixture to a boil; cook over low heat 5 minutes, stirring occasionally. Spread on lamb during last 10 to 15 minutes of cooking.
Seasonings	Suggested seasonings for lamb: basil leaves, rosemary leaves, thyme, garlic, ground ginger and curry powder.

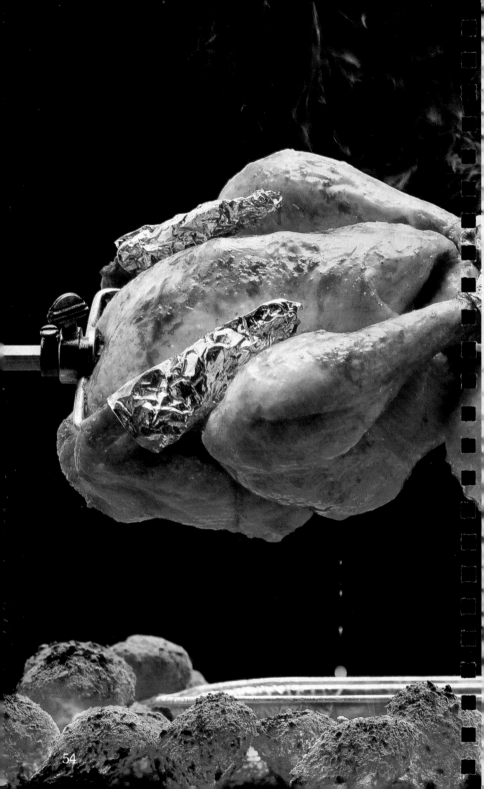

Poultry

Poultry Pointers

Chicken

Chicken has everything going for it: it's nutritious, low in fat and calories, and economical. But other kinds of poultry are delicious when barbecued, too.

Game hens, ducklings and turkeys all can be roasted over the coals or grilled to make great eating for family or company meals. For best results, cook poultry over medium to low coals and baste it thoroughly and often. Marinating enhances flavor and adds variety. An aluminum foil drip pan prevents burned skin, and saves juices for meat gravy.

Open Brazier. Grill chicken parts over medium, direct heat. Turn every 10 minutes to ensure even cooking.

Turkey

Whole Turkey. Grill in a covered cooker over indirect heat. Save time; cook two small turkeys instead of one. Brush with liquid hickory smoke.

Covered Cooker. For smoked flavor in a covered cooker add hickory chips and liquid smoke to the coals. Place the poultry on grid opposite coals. Keep the cover closed and use low heat. Turn occasionally.

Game Hens

Game Hens. Grill over medium, indirect heat. Baste hen inside and out with herb butter. Cook breast side up, covered, with vents open. Baste often.

Covered Cooker. Grill chicken parts, quarters and halves over medium, direct heat. Cooking time will be shortened and smoked barbecued flavor will be stronger than in an open brazier.

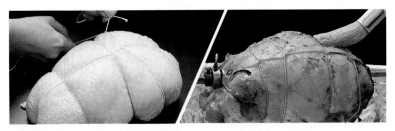

Turkey Breast. Grill for an inexpensive low calorie, low cholesterol entrée. Thaw; tie with clean string to form an even shape, pictured above left. Thread on spit; brush with butter and baste with sauce, page 28. Roast over medium, indirect heat, pictured above right.

Duck

Duckling. Grill over medium, indirect heat in a covered cooker. For quartered ducklings turn every 10 minutes, pictured above left. For whole ducklings score skin for self-basting and place in roasting rack, pictured above right. Brush with soy sauce for added flavor.

How to Rotisserie Poultry

Wash and season bird. Don't stuff birds to be grilled on rotisserie, just use herb butter and seasonings. Grill stuffing separately. See page 60 for directions.

Tie wings and legs securely to body to prevent flopping. Skewer neck skin to back. It's easiest to truss birds before mounting on spit.

Thread one prong onto spit and run the spit from the neck to the tail of bird. When bird is in position, insert second prong and secure tightly.

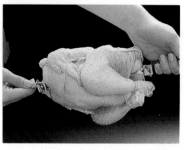

Test balance by rotating spit in hand. If bird is flopping on spit, re-thread and tighten prongs. Rotate again.

Mount several birds on one spit by butting them head to tail. Try small game hens, chicken, turkey. Be sure to tie all wings and legs. Rotate by hand for balance check. Be sure to use enough coals to cook thoroughly.

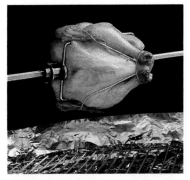

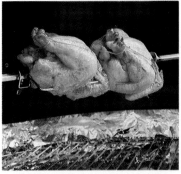

One bird balances best if spit is slightly toward backbone of bird, since breast cavity is hollow. Place bird in center of spit.

Two birds should be of similar size and shape for best balance. Poor balance will affect browning because they won't rotate smoothly on the spit.

How to Bundle Wrap a Chicken Dinner

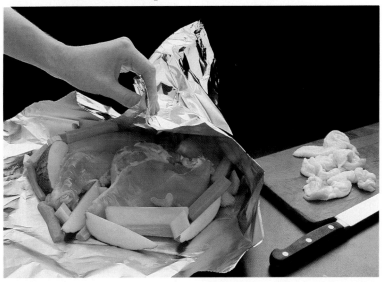

Bundle Wrap chicken in an aluminum foil packet. Remove skin for low calorie combinations; debone for an easy no mess meal; then add garden fresh vegetables with your favorite herbs or sauce. Grill over medium, direct heat 30 to 40 minutes.

Remove with tongs and open carefully. Expect steaming. Sprinkle with Parmesan cheese before serving. Serve directly from aluminum foil packet.

How to Combination-Cook Poultry

Grill twice the amount of poultry pieces you need for one meal. Freeze extras in Heavy Duty Reynolds Wrap.®

Unwrap chicken. Defrost and warm in microwave. Chicken will taste and look freshly grilled.

Reverse method. While starting coals, micro-cook larger cuts of poultry for half of recommended time. Finish on grill.

How to Cook Stuffing While Grilling Poultry

Bundle Wrap favorite stuffing in a double thickness of aluminum foil. Add several drops of water to prevent drying out.

Place aluminum foil packet on edge of grid, away from hot center of coals. Grill 15 to 20 minutes or until heated through.

Remove aluminum foil packet from grill and serve stuffing with a spoonful or two of juices from drip pan for extra flavor.

Tips for Grilling Poultry

1. Season birds for better flavor. Try hickory salt, garlic powder, paprika, pepper and parsley or your favorite combination.

2. Cook all poultry to an internal temperature of 185°F. For birds high in fat, such as duck, make certain drip pan is positioned to catch all drippings to prevent flare-ups.

3. Test poultry for doneness. Grill poultry until it is well done and flesh is no longer pink. Meat thermometer should read 185°F, and fork can be inserted with ease.

Poultry Chart

Cook all poultry over medium, indirect heat except for broiler-fryer parts and quarters, which use medium, direct heat.

Type of Poultry	Time in Covered Grill	Time on Rotisserie	Time on Open Brazier
Broiler-Fryer:			
Whole 2½ to 3½ lbs.	1¼ to 1½ hrs.	1½ to 2 hrs.	*
Parts	30 to 35 min.	*	35 to 40 min.
Quarters	40 to 50 min.	*	30 to 40 min.
Cornish Hens			
Whole 1½ lbs.	30 to 40 min.	1 to 1½ hrs.	*
Domestic Duck			
Whole 4 to 5 lbs.	1¾ to 2¼ hrs.	2½ to 3 hrs.	*
Quarters	1 to 1¼ hrs.	*	*
Turkey			
Whole 8 to 12 lbs.	1½ to 2 hrs.	2 to 3 hrs.	*
Whole 12 to 16 lbs.	2 to 2½ hrs.	*	*
Breast 5 to 8 lbs.	1½ to 2½ hrs.	2½ to 3 hrs.	*

*This method not recommended.

Poultry Variations

Name/Yield	Ingredients
Cornish Hens 4 servings	1 pkg. (6¼ oz.) quick-cooking long grain and wild rice ½ lb. pork sausage 1 cup chopped onion ½ cup chopped celery 4 Cornish hens

Grilled Duckling
and a side of sauce
4 servings
	1 4- to 5-lb. domestic duck
	1 can (15¼ oz.) pineapple
	    chunks, drained
	1 can (11 oz.) mandarin
	    oranges, drained
	1 medium green pepper, cut
	    into rings
	1 pkg. (2 oz.) sweet and sour
	    sauce mix
	⅓ cup water
	3 tablespoons vinegar

Bundle-Wrapped
Chicken Dinner
4 servings
	8 chicken parts
	2 cups sliced summer squash
	4 slices cooked, crumbled
	    bacon
	2 envelopes instant single
	    serving onion soup
	Dairy sour cream

Poultry Kabobs with
Stir-Fried Vegetables
4 servings
	½ cup soy sauce
	2 tablespoons brown sugar
	¼ teaspoon ground ginger
	¼ teaspoon garlic powder
	4 to 5 cups fresh vegetables,
	    bite-size chunks
	4 skewers of poultry kabobs,
	    page 77

Turkey Breast with
Vegetable Casserole
8 servings
	1 pkg. (10 oz.) frozen broccoli
	    spears
	1 medium onion, parboiled
	    and quartered
	1 can (11 oz.) Cheddar cheese
	    soup
	¼ cup milk
	½ cup soft bread crumbs
	2 tablespoons melted butter

Method	Cooking Time
Prepare rice according to package directions. Cook sausage, celery and onion together in frying pan. Drain. Combine with cooked rice. Stuff hens. Place in 4 foil mini-casserole pans.	25 to 30 min., medium, indirect heat, in covered grill.
Cut duckling into quarters. Combine remaining ingredients in a Reynolds Wrap® saucepan. Spoon sauce over duckling quarters when serving.	**Duckling Quarters:** 1 to 1¼ hours, medium, indirect heat, in covered grill. **Fruit Sauce:** 20 to 30 minutes, in same grill.
Place chicken, squash and bacon on four sheets of aluminum foil. Sprinkle with soup. Bundle wrap. Spoon on sour cream when serving.	40 min., medium, direct heat, in open brazier.
Combine soy sauce, brown sugar, ginger and garlic. Toss half of sauce with vegetables. Stir-fry with 1 teaspoon cooking oil in foil pan. Place kabobs around edge of grill. Baste with the remaining sauce.	**Vegetables:** 10 min., hot, direct heat, stirring frequently. **Kabobs:** 15 to 20 min., medium, indirect heat, turning once.
Partially defrost broccoli and cut into 1-inch pieces. Place in foil square cake pan with onion. Combine soup and milk. Add to vegetables. Top with combined bread crumbs and butter. Cover with aluminum foil.	**Turkey Breast:** 1½ to 2 hr., medium, indirect heat, in covered grill. **Casserole:** 25 to 30 min., medium, indirect heat. (Remove aluminum foil cover last 10 min.)

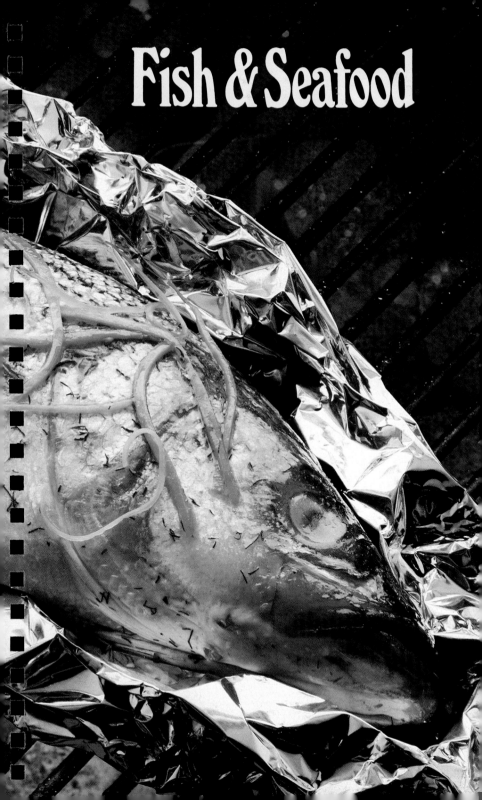

Fish & Seafood

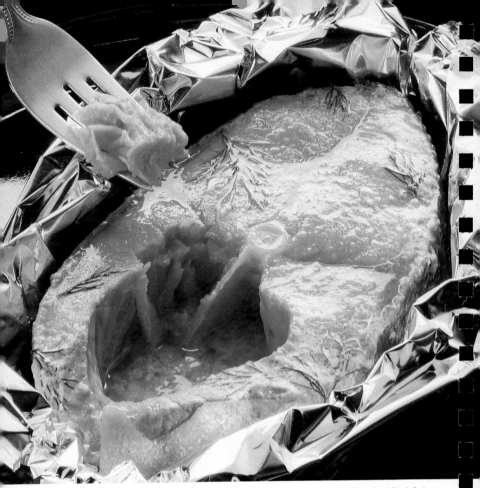

Poached Red Salmon

Fish

There's a way to grill every kind of fish and seafood available. Firmer fleshed fish steaks like salmon and swordfish can be marinated then grilled quickly over the coals.

Remember to support delicate fish like brook trout with a wire basket or aluminum foil loop. Larger, whole fish can be stuffed and steamed over the coals by wrapping in Heavy Duty Reynolds Wrap.® Basting enhances fish flavor. Be sure to baste lean fish like whitefish to prevent drying. Basting is not necessary with fattier fish like bluefish or mackerel but can add flavor.

Cooking your fish to perfection is easy on the grill. Don't overcook. *Never* overhandle!

How to Know if Fish is Done

Fin. Tug gently on side (pectoral) fin. If it comes away easily, fish is done. If not, grill additional 5 to 10 minutes.

Juices. If the juices run clear when fish is pricked and flesh can be flaked with fork, the fish is done.

Flesh. Fish is done when flesh is opaque and there are no traces of pinkness remaining near the backbone.

How to Poach Fish in Individual Aluminum Foil Packets

Tear off a sheet of Heavy Duty Reynolds Wrap® large enough for adequate wrapping; grease. Place ½- to ¾-pound small whole fish, steak or single layer of fillets on aluminum foil.

Season fish with salt, pepper, paprika and parsley. Combine 2 tablespoons water, 1 tablespoon melted butter and 1 tablespoon lemon juice or dry white wine; pour over fish.

Seal with Bundle Wrap, page 25. Place 4 to 5 inches over medium-hot coals. Cook according to Grilling Time, page 71.

How to Bake Fish in Aluminum Foil Packets

Grease center of sheet of heavy duty aluminum foil. Place a layer of sliced lemon on center of aluminum foil. Top lemon slices with whole fish, fish steaks or fish fillets.

Season fish with celery salt, pepper, onion powder, parsley and melted butter. If desired, layer fillets or stuff cavity of whole fish with sliced or shredded vegetables.

Seal with Drugstore Wrap, page 25. Place packet 4 to 5 inches over medium-hot coals. Cook according to Grilling Time, page 71.

How to Stuff and Cook Whole Fish

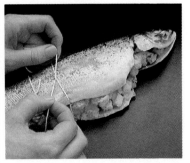

Clean and dress fish. Rub inside with seasonings. Fill fish loosely with seasoned bread or rice stuffing. Bind with clean string or foil loops, page 70. Cook using covered grill or the open brazier method.

Covered Grill Method. Place in greased Reynolds Wrap® baking pan, page 14. Top with melted butter and lemon slices. Cook in covered grill over medium-hot coals according to Grilling Time, page 71.

Open Brazier Method. Drugstore Wrap fish to cook on open brazier. Cook over medium-hot coals according to Grilling Time, page 71.

How to Grill Fish in Hinged Grill Basket

Use a long-handled hinged grill basket for grilling more delicate fillets, steaks and small whole fish. Basket will make turning easier and faster.

Season or marinate fish for 30 minutes before grilling. Place in oiled wire basket. Brush with marinade or melted butter; top one side with thin lemon slice.

Place basket with fish 4 to 5 inches over medium-hot coals. Sear one side and turn to finish. Brush with marinade or melted butter during cooking to prevent drying.

How to Grill Fish in Flat Spit Basket

Clean small whole fish. Leave skin on. Season cavity of fish with melted butter, salt, pepper and herbs.

Oil a flat spit basket with vegetable oil or oil-based salad dressing. Gently lay fish side-by-side in basket. Close basket tightly, being careful not to crush fish.

Center basket on spit. Basket should be directly over medium-hot coals at rotisserie height. Turn on rotisserie; baste fish once during cooking.

How to Make Reynolds Wrap Loops

Tear off a 12-inch length of Heavy Duty Reynolds Wrap.® Fold in half lengthwise four times to make a strip ¾ inch wide. Grease one side of strip and place under fish.

Fold in half with ends meeting above the fish. Fold ends together in locked folds until snug against fish.

Twist once to secure loop and form handle for turning. Turn fish over with mitts, using loop handles. (Use one loop for fish steaks and two for large fish.)

How to Grill Fish Directly on Grid

Select firm-fleshed and sturdy-skinned whole fish or fish steaks to grill directly on grid. Marinate fish steaks 30 minutes before cooking, if desired. Wrap loops around fish.

Oil grid generously. Place fish 4 to 5 inches over medium-hot coals. Use covered or brazier grill. Brush with marinade or melted butter during cooking.

Turn fish with Reynolds Wrap loops halfway through cooking time. Cook according to Grilling Time, page 71.

Baked Fish with Vegetables

Grilling Time for Fish

Measure raw fish, stuffed fish or fish roll-ups at thickest point. If fish is placed 4 inches from medium-hot coals, grilling time will be in basket, on grid or in covered grill, 10 minutes per inch; if foil-wrapped, 15 minutes per inch.

Fish Recipe Chart

Type	Method
Stuffing for Whole Fish	To add additional flavor and zest to whole fish, fill cavity with lemon herb stuffing. Prepare herb-seasoned stuffing mix according to package directions. Add parsley, grated lemon peel, basil and garlic to taste. Top stuffed fish with melted butter, lemon juice and thinly sliced onion rings. To grill see page 68.
Baked Fish with Vegetables	Sprinkle cavity of whole fish with salt and pepper. Tie with clean string. Place in greased aluminum foil pan. Sauté sliced onion and chopped garlic in butter; add basil leaves, parsley and chopped fresh or canned and drained tomatoes or favorite sliced vegetable. Pour over fish. Top with cooked, crumbled bacon. Cook in covered grill 4 to 5 inches over medium-hot coals.
Baked Fish with Herbs and Lemon	Salt and pepper fish steaks, fillets or whole fish. Place fish on heavy duty aluminum foil. Sprinkle with dill weed, or favorite herb, chopped green onion and 1 tablespoon sherry or melted butter. Top with sliced lemon. Seal with Drugstore Wrap, page 25. Cook on grid 4 to 5 inches over medium-hot coals.

71

Seafood

Shrimp

Place six medium cleaned shrimp on Heavy Duty Reynolds Wrap.® Sprinkle with salt and pepper, add 2 tablespoons Garlic Butter, page 29. Bundle Wrap. Grill over medium, direct heat 10 to 12 minutes.

Butterfly a larger shrimp or use smaller shelled deveined whole shrimp. Grill over low coals until pink and firm, about 5 minutes. Brush often with marinade. Do not overcook.

If you have access to fresh seafood, your barbecue pleasures are multiplied. Seafood requires little in the way of pre-preparation and takes very little time over the coals. It's appetizing when cooked "au natural" and rises to sublime heights when marinated and/or sauced. You can serve seafood appetizers before a main course of beef or chicken or make a meal of a mixed seafood grill. If the big grill is busy cooking roast, why not bring out an extra hibachi or portable grill and let guests toast their own shrimp or crab legs?

Lobster

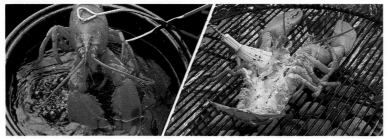

Lobster. Place live lobster head first into rapidly boiling water. Remove when water re-boils. Split and clean, pictured above left. Brush with herb butter, page 29. Grill 3 inches from medium coals, shell down, for about 10 minutes. Turn and grill for an additional 5 minutes or until done, pictured above right.

Rock Lobster Tails and Crab

Thaw lobster tails before grilling. Snip off thin shell on flesh side. Bend backward to crack shell in several places.

Baste with butter. Place shell side down on grill. Barbecue 10 minutes, basting often.

Turn and grill 5 minutes more until flesh is opaque and flakes easily. Serve with lemon and melted butter.

Crab. Defrost King crab legs. Split; remove top half of shell. Baste with Italian dressing. Grill flesh up 5 inches from medium heat 10 minutes. Turn and grill 5 more minutes or until done.

Kabobs

Plan ingredients for a kabob cookout with an idea of what flavors complement each other. Set up skewers so that when juices intermingle, new interesting flavors result. Most basic skewers are stainless steel; use potholders or mitts to turn these. Better yet are two-pronged or square skewers, since they prevent flopping. For good function, use skewers with wooden handles which are easy to hold and turn. Use more than one kind of marinade in a meal.

How to Prepare Food for Skewers

Chunks. Cut meats and vegetables into bite-size chunks or rounds for easiest handling.

Strips. Weave meat strips 1 inch wide and ¼ inch thick onto skewer accordion-style. Place fruits and vegetables in loops. Turn kabobs frequently.

Wedges. Use sweet onions, green peppers, eggplant, potatoes, cantaloupe and fresh pineapple. Tuck the smaller cut wedges into larger ones.

Whole Foods. They retain identity, have eye appeal. Skewer scallops, cocktail franks, cherry tomatoes and whole mushrooms.

Tips for Kabob-ing

Parboil slower cooking foods so grilling times will be same as other foods on the skewer. Parboil small white onions, carrots and chunks of corn-on-the-cob.

Stuff centers of pork and beef balls with water chestnuts, mushrooms, olives or pineapple for best results. Select stuffing, work into center of meatball, then skewer.

Serve individual skewers of meat or vegetables as an appetizer. Soak wooden skewers briefly in water. Assemble food on skewer. Marinate, turning once. Grill.

Prepare separate skewers of vegetables so that they will not be overcooked when grilling chunks of meat and poultry at the same time.

Wrap cooked kabob skewers in Heavy Duty Reynolds Wrap® to keep warm until serving time.

Marinate 3 to 4 hours to ensure tenderness for economical, less tender cuts of meat.

77

Kabob Chart

Type	Time, direct heat	Method
Beef		
Sirloin 1½-inch cubes ¼-inch strips	Medium-hot 12 to 14 min. 8 to 10 min.	Grill, turning frequently.
Round 1½-inch cubes	8 to 12 min.	Marinate 3 to 4 hours in Beer Marinade, page 27. Grill, turning frequently.
Chuck 1¼- to 1½-inch cubes	10 to 12 min.	Same as above.
Ground Beef Stuffed meatballs 1½-inch	Medium-hot 15 to 17 min.	Use water chestnuts, whole mushrooms, pickles or olives as center of meatball. Turn often.
Fish and Seafood Shrimp green, peeled, deveined (medium size)	Medium 4 to 5 min.	Grill, turning often. Brush with melted butter seasoned with lemon and garlic.
Scallops		Same as above.
Lamb Leg or Shoulder 1¼-inch cubes	Medium 13 to 16 min.	Marinate 3 to 4 hours in Apple Tarragon Marinade, page 27. Grill, turning frequently.
Sausage Polish sausage ¾-inch cubes	Medium 13 to 15 min.	Grill, turning often.
Bratwurst ¾-inch cubes	15 to 18 min.	Grill, turning often.

Type	Time, direct heat	Method
Pork		
Loin 1¼-inch cubes	Medium-low 15 to 18 min.	Grill, turning frequently. Brush with Hot and Spicy Sauce, page 28, during last 10 minutes of cooking time.
Shoulder 1¼-inch cubes	14 to 16 min.	Marinate 3 to 4 hours in Pineapple Marinade, page 27. Grill, turning frequently.
Ground Pork		
Stuffed meatballs 1½-inch	Medium-hot 15 to 17 min.	Use water chestnuts, green pepper chunks or pineapple chunks as center of meatball. Grill, turning often. Brush with bottled Teriyaki sauce.
Poultry		
Chicken 1-inch chunks ¼-inch strips	Medium-hot 15 to 18 min. 13 to 15 min.	Grill, turning frequently. Brush with melted butter or marinate in Teriyaki Marinade, page 27.
Chicken livers	8 to 10 min.	Thread with bacon strips. Grill. Turn often.
Turkey 1¼- to 1½-inch chunks	18 to 20 min.	Grill. Turn often. Brush with melted butter, season with salt, pepper and paprika before serving or brush with Hot and Spicy Sauce, page 28, during last 10 minutes of cooking.
Fruit		
Cubes	Medium 5 to 8 min.	Grill until warm but not brown. Baste with Cinnamon Butter or a sauce, page 28, 29.
Vegetables		Refer to Vegetable Chart, page 84

Vegetables

Experiment with grilling and you will develop some vegetable specialties. Favorite recipes for the range and oven can be done in a covered grill if you allow extra time for baking. Vegetables buttered, seasoned and wrapped in Heavy Duty Reynolds Wrap® then grilled, retain wonderful steamed-in flavor and have an appealing texture.

There are five basic methods for grilling vegetables: ember cooking, foil wrapping, directly on grid, skewered, and stir-fried. Try any one of these methods on an open grill, in a covered unit or in a charcoal water smoker.

How to Foil Wrap

Drugstore Wrap potatoes or similar vegetables. Place on edge of grid on a covered grill while cooking a roast. Turn potatoes several times while cooking. To serve, cut open and add desired topping.

Stuffed Potato, page 86　　81

How to Ember Cook

Ember cook hard vegetables like acorn squash and sweet potatoes right in coals, with or without a foil wrap. Oil the skins before placing in coals.

Drugstore Wrap is desirable for ember cooking since it permits turning. To prevent charring chunked vegetables like zucchini, green peppers, or onions, wrap in double thickness of heavy duty aluminum foil.

Foil Wrap more delicately skinned vegetables. For corn, remove the silk, keeping the husk. Soak in ice water and Drugstore Wrap. Turn frequently for even cooking.

How to Skewer Cook Vegetables

Cut vegetables into bite-size wedges or chunks. Alternate shapes for variety. The thinner the vegetable is cut, the more quickly it will cook.

Skewer vegetables alternating with meat chunks or strips. Strips of beef can shield more delicate vegetables like tomatoes and mushrooms. Brush with soy/teriyaki sauce and grill.

All vegetable skewers should be threaded with similar sizes and shapes of vegetables to promote more even cooking. Skewer zucchini and yellow squash; mushrooms and green peppers; onions and potatoes; sweet potatoes and pineapple.

How to Grill Directly on Grid

Parboil root vegetables and cook directly on the grid over medium coals turning frequently. Baste with seasoned butter.

Halve summer squash lengthwise, brush with butter and grill in hinged basket. Oil basket to prevent sticking. Grill over medium, direct heat 15 to 20 minutes. Turn frequently.

Bundle Wrap a variety of vegetables. As a side dish for your favorite steak, Bundle Wrap individual servings of onions, mushrooms, green peppers and seasonings. Use medium, direct heat.

Cover cut edge of halved vegetables with Heavy Duty Reynolds Wrap® to prevent charring. Grill cut side down first. Turn halfway through cooking time.

How to Stir Fry Over the Coals

Place large wok directly over the coals or on grid over coals. Use ring for balance. Some grills come with wok that fits directly into grill. Use long-handled tongs or wooden spoon to stir quickly.

Vegetable Chart

Vegetable	Method	Preparation
Beans, Green	Drugstore Wrap	Cut diagonally.
Carrots	Drugstore Wrap	Scrub, don't peel. Discard ends.
	On grid	Parboil 3 min.
Corn Whole	*Ember	Remove silk, leaving husk. Soak in water.
	Drugstore Wrap	Remove husks and silk.
Cut	Bundle Wrap	Cut corn off cob.
Chunks	Kabobs	Parboil 3 min.
Mush- rooms	Bundle Wrap	Cut off stems.
	Kabobs	Cut off stems.
Onions	*Ember	Remove ends.
	Kabobs	Parboil 3 min.
Peppers	Kabobs	Cut in 1½-inch chunks.
Potatoes, Sweet or Baking	*Ember	Oil whole vegetable.
	Drugstore Wrap	
Halves	On grid	Cover cut sides with aluminum foil.
Slices	Bundle Wrap	Slice very thin. Spread in even layer.
Cubes	Kabobs	Peeled, 1¼-inch.
New	On grid	Scrub.
Summer Squash	Bundle Wrap	Slices, lengthwise.
	Kabobs	1¼-inch chunks.
	Grill basket	Slices, lengthwise.
Tomatoes, Halves	Bundle Wrap	Cut in half.
Cherry	Kabobs	Leave whole.

*Ember cook — wrap vegetables in heavy duty aluminum foil or place directly on coals.

Seasoning	Time/Min.	Direct Heat
Almonds, butter and a few tablespoons water	20 to 25	medium
Butter, basil and a few tablespoons water	25	medium
Herbed butter	35 to 40	medium-low
—	35 to 45	low, turn often
Butter, salt, pepper and a few tablespoons water	45	medium
Chopped onion, green pepper and tomato	20	medium
Melted butter	5 to 10	medium
Butter, salt and pepper	15 to 20	medium
Melted butter	6 to 8	medium
—	45	low, turn often
Melted butter	20	medium
Melted butter	12 to 15	medium
—	45 to 55	low, turn often
	55 to 60	low
—	60	medium, turn once
Butter, salt, pepper	45	medium-hot
Melted butter	35 to 40	medium-hot
Melted butter	40 to 50	medium
Salt, pepper and butter	20	medium
Italian salad dressing	12 to 15	medium
Melted butter	15 to 20	medium
Butter, Parmesan cheese and parsley	30 to 40	medium
Melted butter.	5	medium

Stuffed Vegetable Meals

For optimum results, wrap stuffed vegetables in aluminum foil and cook in a covered grill. However, foil wrapped vegetables can be cooked on an open grill but will require additional time.

How to Stuff Vegetables

Stuffed Potato. Slit potato at ¼-inch intervals. Do not cut all the way through. Place onion slices, seasoned salt, garlic powder, celery salt, pepper and butter in slits. Top with sliced mushrooms. Drugstore Wrap. Grill over hot, direct heat 55 to 60 minutes. To serve, open packet and top with cooked bacon, Parmesan cheese, tomatoes and parsley.

Stuffed Tomato. Hollow out; drain. Fill with frozen peas, slightly thawed, green onion, Parmesan cheese, salt, pepper and melted butter. Bundle Wrap. Cook in a covered grill over medium, indirect heat 35 minutes.

Stuffed Yellow Squash. Hollow out. Chop pulp; sauté in butter with onion, garlic and chopped spinach. Mix with mozzarella and Parmesan cheese. Spoon into squash. Drugstore Wrap. Cook in a covered grill over medium, indirect heat 20 minutes.

Stuffed Sweet Onion. Hollow out. Fill with frozen spinach soufflé, slightly thawed. Bundle Wrap. Cook in a covered grill over medium, indirect heat 50 minutes. Open packet during last 5 minutes.

How to Stuff Eggplant

Cut tops lengthwise from two eggplants. Scoop out insides of eggplants, leaving ½-inch wall. Place shells on sheet of Heavy Duty Reynolds Wrap.®

Chop pulp of eggplants; sauté in butter with onion, zucchini, tomatoes, garlic and olives. Combine with cooked rice and spaghetti sauce.

Spoon into eggplant shells. Drugstore Wrap. Cook over medium, indirect heat in a covered grill 35 minutes or until heated through.

Breads & Desserts

Breads

The foil-wrapped loaf has many variations from grilled garlic bread to a savory herb dilled bread. For added interest, serve these breads with some of the seasoned butters listed on page 29. Pre-baked breads and frozen rolls are another convenient barbecue menu addition. Foil wrap them according to the directions on page 25.

How to Grill Rolls and Bread

Brown-and-Serve Rolls. Place rolls in foil pan. Bake in covered grill over medium-low, indirect heat 4 to 5 minutes or until evenly browned.

Sandwich Chart

Type	Method
Stuffed Stromboli	Cut ¼ inch off top of Kaiser roll. Hollow out center. Stuff with layers of salami, Provolone cheese, pepperoni and sautéed green pepper and onion. Cover with top. Drugstore Wrap in aluminum foil. Grill over medium coals, turning frequently until heated through.
Grilled Open-Faced Sandwich	Butter both sides of slice of pumpernickel bread. Spread top side with Dijon mustard. Layer with corned beef, finely chopped onion, caraway seeds and Swiss cheese. Place in foil pan or Reynolds Wrap baking pan, page 14. Place on covered grill. Cook over medium coals until heated through.
Pocket Bread Sand-wiches	Marinate beef strips in Teriyaki Marinade, page 27. Weave beef strips around green pepper chunks and thick wedges of onion and thread on skewers. Grill according to Kabob Chart, page 78. Cut ½ inch off top of pocket bread. Seal with Drugstore Wrap; place on grill until heated through. To serve, empty skewers into pocket bread.
Ham and Cheese Loaf	Cut French bread loaf diagonally at ¾-inch intervals, almost to bottom crust. Combine ½ cup butter, softened, ½ cup grated Cheddar cheese, 1 cup finely chopped ham, 1 teaspoon celery seed and 2 tablespoons chopped onion; spread filling between slices. Drugstore Wrap in aluminum foil. Grill over medium-hot coals, 20 minutes or until heated through; turn often.

 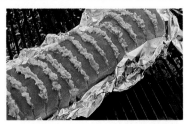

Garlic Bread. Slash a loaf of French or Italian bread almost through in ¾-inch intervals. Spread garlic butter between slices. Drugstore Wrap in aluminum foil. Grill 20 minutes over medium-hot coals; turn often.

Sandwich Loaf. Slash loaf as described and spread with cheese, ham, tuna or chicken salad. Drugstore Wrap in aluminum foil. Grill 20 minutes over medium-hot coals; turn often.

Desserts

Hot Grill Desserts

Desserts on the grill can range from skewered fruit brushed with honey and lemon to pies and baked apples. Old-fashioned s'mores can be made conveniently and in advance for a traditional barbecue favorite with children. Simply sandwich a chocolate square and marshmallow creme between two graham crackers. Drugstore Wrap in heavy duty aluminum foil and grill until chocolate is melted.

Baked Apple. Core apples. Fill with raisins, coconut, brown sugar, and cinnamon. Bundle Wrap. Grill over medium, direct heat in a covered grill 20 minutes until tender.

Pineapple Kabobs. Pare and cut fresh pineapple into wedges. Thread on skewers and grill over medium heat 5 minutes basting with a combination of honey, butter and cinnamon.

Pie. Heat a freshly made fruit crisp or pie in a covered grill. Prepare in aluminum foilware pan. Overwrap by using Bundle Wrap and grill over coals until steaming. Serve warm with ice cream.

91

Barbecued appetizers and snacks are the perfect thing to serve while guests relax before dinner or as a late night snack around the fireplace. They can be prepared with almost any type of barbecue grill.

Grill baskets work well with small foods like miniature chicken wings and simplify turning many small pieces at one time.

For late night snacking, try nachos over the coals. Prepare according to directions below. Many convenience foods like frozen egg rolls can be done in a covered grill. Experiment with some of your favorites. Check package directions.

How to Grill Appetizers and Snacks

Popcorn. Place 3 tablespoons popping corn and 1 tablespoon oil in center of a double thickness of heavy duty aluminum foil. Bundle Wrap, leaving expansion room. Grill over hot, direct heat; shake with long-handled tongs until popping stops.

Nachos. Place corn tortilla chips on a foil toaster oven tray. Top with chopped green chili peppers and Monterey Jack cheese. Cover with aluminum foil tent. Grill over medium, direct heat until melted, 10 to 12 minutes.

Appetizers & Snacks

Nachos

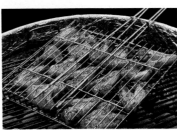

Barbecued Party Wings. Remove and discard bony tips of chicken wings. Marinate in Teriyaki Marinade, page 27, then grill slowly in grill basket 45 minutes or until crusty brown. Terrific finger food!

Oysters and Clams. Shuck and drain, then place in deep halves of shells. Prepare favorite clam stuffing. Grill over hot, direct coals 12 to 15 minutes or until bubbly.

Index